Rise After the Fall

Moving On with Strength and Grace

PRADUMNA VERMA

Contents

Foreword

Heartbreak is a universal experience—an inevitable chapter in the book of life. It is a journey filled with questions, confusion, and a deep longing to understand why things fell apart. During this time, it's easy to feel isolated, as if the pain is uniquely your own. But here's the truth: you are not alone, and within every ending lies the seed of a new beginning.

"Rise After the Fall" was born from the realization that we all carry the strength within us to heal and grow, even in our darkest moments. This book is not just a guide; it's a companion. It's for anyone who has ever felt lost in the ruins of a broken relationship and wondered if they could ever rebuild. It's a reminder that while the journey may be difficult, it is also an opportunity for transformation, self-love, and rediscovery.

I wrote this book because I've been there—I've faced the emptiness, the silent nights, and the overwhelming urge to hold onto the past. But I've also witnessed the beauty that comes with embracing change and choosing to move forward. My hope is that these pages will offer you comfort, perspective, and the gentle nudge you need to rise again.

This isn't just about letting go—it's about moving on with grace, reclaiming your power, and finding joy in life once more. Let this book be your guide as you take those first steps toward healing, and may it remind you that after every fall, you have the strength to rise.

With compassion and hope,

Pradumna Verma

Acknowledgments

Writing "Rise After the Fall: Moving On with Strength and Grace" has been a deeply personal journey, and I could not have completed it without the support and encouragement of several people who have been by my side.

First and foremost, I am eternally grateful to my family. To my mother, whose unwavering love and wisdom have always been my guiding light—thank you for teaching me resilience and for always believing in me.

A heartfelt thank you to my friends who stood by me during my own difficult moments. Your understanding and kindness have been invaluable.

I also want to express my appreciation to those whose silent presence in my life provided the lessons that inspired many of the words in this book. Even though our paths may no longer cross, your impact remains.

A special thanks to my readers—your trust and willingness to open your hearts and heal is what makes this journey meaningful. My hope is that this book offers you the comfort, strength, and guidance you seek.

Finally, to everyone who believes in the power of healing, growth, and the possibility of new beginnings, this book is for you.

With deepest gratitude,

Pradumna Verma

Introduction

A Journey Through Heartbreak and Healing

We've all been there—the late nights staring at the ceiling, the endless replay of memories, the *"what if"* scenarios that keep circling in our minds. Breakups have a way of shaking us to our core, leaving us feeling lost and empty. Whether it was the love of your life or a fleeting romance, the pain feels real, raw, and overwhelming. You might feel as if no one truly understands what you're going through, or that no words can soothe the ache.

This book is not here to tell you to *"get over it"* or to move on as if it were that simple. I know it isn't. Moving on is a journey—a process of rediscovering yourself, reclaiming your peace, and finding hope again in the cracks of what's been shattered. It's about embracing the pain, learning from it, and slowly letting it transform you into someone stronger, wiser, and more in tune with yourself.

Why This Book?

I wrote this book for everyone who feels stuck in the cycle of heartache. I've been where you are now. I know what it's like to feel like a prisoner to your own thoughts, to carry the weight of loss like an invisible burden. This is not just a guide, but a companion to walk with you through your emotions, to remind you that healing is messy, nonlinear, and unique to each person.

Through a mix of stories, heartfelt advice, practical exercises, and a sprinkle of poetry, I aim to show you that moving on doesn't have to be a lonely, painful process. You can heal with grace, find joy in the little things, and most importantly, rediscover who you are without the shadow of the past holding you back.

A New Beginning

This book is not just about the end of a relationship; it's about the beginning of something beautiful—yourself. As you turn these pages, I hope you find comfort, encouragement, and the strength to believe that brighter days are ahead. Together, we'll explore how to let go, how to heal, and how to fall back in love—with life, and with yourself.

Welcome to your journey of moving on. It won't be easy, but I promise you it will be worth it.

Chapter 1: Understanding Your Pain

Breakups leave a unique kind of scar. It's a pain that doesn't just touch the heart—it reaches deep into your soul, tugging at your very sense of self. The end of a relationship isn't just the loss of a person; it's the loss of a shared world, of dreams, of a version of yourself that existed only with them. You may feel like you've lost not just love, but a piece of yourself, and that's what makes it so hard to let go.

In this moment, it's okay to feel fragile. It's okay to feel like you're breaking in ways you didn't know were possible. Heartbreak isn't just about the end of a relationship—it's about the shattered hopes, the broken trust, and the void that seems impossible to fill. But let's start by accepting that this pain is part of the process, part of the story that will one day lead you to a better version of yourself.

The Stages of Grief in Heartbreak

When we think of grief, we often associate it with losing someone to death, but the grief of a breakup is just as real and profound. There's denial, where you wake up hoping it's all a bad dream; anger, where the hurt turns into frustration at yourself, at them, at the universe for letting this happen. Then comes bargaining, those late-night thoughts of *"What if I had d one things differently?"* or *"Maybe I can win them back."* And finally, there's the crushing weight of sadness, when everything feels numb, and you wonder if you'll ever feel whole again.

But after all of this, there's acceptance—not the "I'm fine" kind, but the quiet, almost peaceful realization that while it hurts, it's something you will survive. You start to see glimmers of light in the darkness, small moments of clarity where you realize that healing is happening, even if it's slow and uneven.

Why Does It Hurt So Much?

Have you ever wondered why breakups hurt so deeply? It's not just about missing someone; it's about the identity you built with them. In relationships, we often intertwine our sense of self with our partner. We create stories around us, plans that are built on we, and when that shared vision crumbles, it feels like our very foundation is being pulled out from under us.

This pain is a sign of how much you cared, how deeply you loved. And while that makes it hurt more now, it also shows the capacity your heart has for love, for connection. Remember, the depth of your current pain is a reflection of the depth of your past love. And that's something to honor, even if it feels like a curse right now.

Embracing the Emptiness

Sometimes, the hardest part is the silence. The empty space they used to fill. The quiet moments that now feel unbearably loud because they're gone. But what if, instead of running from that emptiness, we leaned into it? What if we allowed ourselves to sit in that discomfort, to truly feel it without trying to numb it away?

It's in this emptiness that we start to reconnect with ourselves. The parts of you that you may have neglected in the relationship are still there, waiting to be rediscovered. The solitude, painful as it may be, is also an invitation—a chance to meet yourself again, to find out who you are when you're not defined by someone else.

Permission to Feel Everything

One of the biggest mistakes people make after a breakup is trying to force themselves to "move on" too quickly. We live in a world that celebrates strength and resilience, but true strength comes from allowing yourself to feel everything—every tear, every pang of longing, every wave of anger. You don't have to pretend you're okay when you're not. You don't have to hide your pain to make others comfortable.

This chapter is a reminder that it's okay to be messy, to be heartbroken, to be human. Healing isn't linear. Some days you might feel like you're making progress, and the next day, you might feel like you're back at square one. That's normal. That's healing. The important thing is to honor where you are right now without rushing the process.

Finding Strength in Broken Pieces

In the quiet of the night, when tears softly fall,
I feel the ache of love's gentle, bitter call.
You were my sun, my moon, my guiding star,
But now I'm left wondering who you really are.

The dreams we built are dust in the wind,
Promises broken, hearts left to mend.
But in this shadow, I find my way,
A little stronger with each passing day.

It's okay to cry, to feel, to break,
To question the choices we both had to make.
But deep inside, a voice still sings,
Of hope, of light, and better things.

So here I stand, not whole, but free,
To rediscover the heart that still beats in me.
For love is lost, but not in vain,
It taught me strength, it showed me pain.

And in this pain, I start to find,
A deeper love that's mine—just mine.

Chapter 2: Letting Go of the Past

Letting go is one of the hardest things you'll ever do. There's a certain comfort in holding on, in replaying those sweet memories, in imagining how things could have been different. But clinging to the past is like trying to hold onto a flame—it only burns you the longer you grasp it. In this chapter, we'll explore why it's so important to release what no longer serves you and how to begin that journey of letting go.

Why We Hold On

We hold on because those memories bring us comfort, even if they hurt. We remember the laughs, the inside jokes, the way their presence felt like home. Sometimes, we hold on because we're afraid to let go. Letting go feels like accepting that it's really over, and that's terrifying. It's as if letting go erases all the love, the time, the dreams, and the moments you shared. But here's the truth: letting go doesn't mean forgetting. It doesn't mean pretending it never happened. It means acknowledging that those moments were real, and now it's time to release them to make room for something new.

Holding onto the past prevents you from seeing the possibilities of the future. It's like driving a car while only looking in the rearview mirror—you'll never get where you're supposed to be if your eyes are glued to what's behind you.

The Weight of Memories

Memories are tricky. Some days they bring a smile to your face, and other days they hit you like a punch in the gut. But the truth is, memories are just that—memories. They're moments frozen in time, no longer real, no longer part of your present. And while they will always be a part of your story, they don't have to define your future.

You might find yourself revisiting old messages, scrolling through pictures, or reliving conversations. It's natural. We do it because it feels like holding onto those memories keeps that connection alive. But eventually, you have to ask yourself: **Are these memories helping me heal, or are they keeping me stuck?**

Letting go of those memories doesn't mean you didn't care. It doesn't diminish the love you once felt. It simply means that you're choosing yourself, your peace, and your future over a past that no longer exists.

Making Peace with the "What Ifs"

One of the biggest obstacles to letting go is the constant question: *What if?* What if I had done something different? What if they change their mind? What if this breakup is a mistake? These "*what ifs*" are like chains that keep you bound to a past you can't change. They keep you in a loop of regret, making it impossible to move forward.

But here's the thing—no amount of analyzing or replaying scenarios will change what's already happened. Life isn't a movie where you can rewrite the script or go back to change a scene. The sooner you accept that, the sooner you can start to free yourself from the burden of the *"what ifs."*

Choosing to Let Go

Letting go is an act of courage. It's a conscious decision to release the grip you have on the past and to embrace the uncertainty of what lies ahead. It's scary because it means stepping into the unknown, but it's also liberating. When you let go, you make space for growth, for healing, and for new experiences that might be even better than what you're leaving behind.

Think of letting go as decluttering your heart. Just like how you clean out your closet to get rid of things that no longer fit, you have to clear out the emotional clutter that no longer aligns with who you're becoming. Letting go isn't about erasing the past; it's about making room for your future.

A Practical Guide to Letting Go

1. Start by Disconnecting

- Remove or hide reminders that keep triggering painful memories. It's okay to unfollow or mute them on social media. You're not being petty—you're protecting your peace.

2. Rewrite Your Story

- Journal about what you've learned from the relationship. Focus on the growth, not just the pain. Turn those experiences into wisdom that will guide you forward.

3. Create New Routines

- Break the habits that remind you of them. Create new routines that bring you joy and comfort—whether it's taking up a new hobby, spending more time with friends, or focusing on self-care.

4. Practice Self-Compassion

- Be kind to yourself during this process. Letting go takes time, and it's okay if you stumble along the way. Healing is not linear, but every step you take, no matter how small, is progress.

In Letting Go, I Find Myself

In quiet moments when shadows fall,
I hear the whispers of what once was ours.
The dreams we built, the promises made,
Now float like leaves in the autumn fade.

I held you close in every thought,
Clinging to the love I sought.
But time has taught my heart to see,
That holding on kept caging me.

There's beauty in the breaking, in the pain,
In letting go to find your name again.
For sometimes love, though deep and true,
Must find its end to let life through.

So now I stand with open hands,
Releasing what I cannot hold.
The past, it fades, like gentle sand,
But in its place, new dreams unfold.

Goodbye, I whisper—not in spite,
But with a heart that seeks the light.
For in letting go, I set you free,
And in the void, I rediscover me.

Chapter 3: Rediscovering Your Self-Worth

After a breakup, it's common to feel like you've lost a part of yourself. The person you once were might feel distant, overshadowed by doubt, insecurity, and the belief that you're somehow "less" without that relationship. But the truth is, your worth has never depended on someone else's love. This chapter is about reclaiming your identity, rediscovering your self-worth, and understanding that you are whole on your own.

The Illusion of Losing Yourself

When you invest so much of yourself into a relationship, it's easy to feel like your identity is tied to that connection. Maybe you defined yourself by the role you played—partner, lover, supporter. But now that role is gone, and you're left wondering, **Who am I without them?**

The truth is, you were someone long before that relationship began, and you'll continue to be someone valuable after it ends. You might feel like you've lost yourself, but this is really an opportunity to rediscover who you are beyond the relationship. You don't need someone else to validate your worth. You are enough, just as you are.

Breaking Free from the Validation Trap

In a relationship, it's natural to seek validation from your partner. We crave approval, affection, and the sense of being valued. But when that relationship ends, it can leave a void where that validation used to be. You might catch yourself doubting your attractiveness, your abilities, or even your value as a person. But remember, your worth is not something that someone else can define or take away.

Self-worth is about recognizing your own value, independent of anyone else's opinions or actions. It's about knowing that you are deserving of love, respect, and happiness—whether you're single, in a relationship, or anywhere in between. It's about understanding that your value doesn't decrease just because someone failed to see it.

Reconnecting with Yourself

Breakups can make you forget the person you used to be before the relationship. It's time to reconnect with that version of you. What were the things that made you happy? What passions, hobbies, and dreams did you once have that you might have set aside? This is the perfect moment to rekindle those interests and rediscover the things that light you up from within.

Start small. Take time for yourself. Whether it's diving back into an old hobby, picking up a new skill, or just spending quiet time reflecting on your journey, these moments of self-care are essential for rebuilding your sense of self. The more you invest in rediscovering who you are, the more your confidence and self-worth will grow.

The Power of Positive Affirmations

Our inner dialogue has a powerful impact on how we view ourselves. After a breakup, that inner voice can become harsh and critical. You might find yourself thinking things like, **I'm not good enough** or **I'll never find someone who loves me.** These thoughts are damaging and untrue. It's time to change the narrative.

Start by practicing positive affirmations. Every day, remind yourself of your strengths and qualities. Say things like, **I am worthy of love and respect. I am enough. I deserve happiness.** At first, these affirmations might feel forced, but over time, they start to shift your mindset. They remind you that your value comes from within.

Surrounding Yourself with Positivity

The people and environment around you play a huge role in how you feel about yourself. After a breakup, it's important to surround yourself with people who lift you up, who remind you of your worth, and who encourage you to grow. Distance yourself from those who bring negativity or make you doubt yourself.

Fill your life with things that inspire positivity. Whether it's reading uplifting books, listening to empowering podcasts, or simply spending time in nature, these influences can help you rebuild your sense of self and remind you of your inherent worth.

A Journey Back to You

This chapter is about one simple truth: you are enough. The end of a relationship does not diminish your value. It does not define your worth. You were whole before, and you are still whole now. This journey of rediscovery is not just about healing from a breakup—it's about rediscovering the beautiful, resilient, and worthy person that you are.

Becoming Whole Again

There was a time I lost my way,

In shadows deep, where I would stay.

I searched for worth in someone's eyes,

But found only echoes and empty skies.

I thought my value slipped away,

When love was lost and turned to gray.

But deep within, beneath the pain,

A spark of hope began to reign.

I am more than moments passed,

More than love that couldn't last.

I am dreams, and light, and fire,

A heart that beats with pure desire.

No longer will I beg or plead,

For someone else to see my need.

For I am whole, I am enough,

In gentle strength, though times were tough.

So now I rise with tender grace,

With tears that fall but leave no trace.

For in my scars, I find my voice,

In my own love, I make my choice.

To cherish all that's found in me,

To let my heart and spirit be free.

For in the end, I've come to see,

I am my own—complete, at peace, and free.

Chapter 4: Embracing Solitude

Solitude can feel like a heavy burden after a breakup. The silence, the empty spaces, and the absence of shared routines can be overwhelming. But there's a difference between loneliness and solitude. Loneliness is the ache for company, while solitude is the comfort found in your own presence. In this chapter, we'll explore how embracing solitude is not just a step toward healing—it's a journey of self-discovery.

From Loneliness to Solitude

At first, being alone can feel like an unbearable void. The sudden shift from having someone there to having only your own company can be jarring. The quiet moments seem too quiet; the nights stretch on endlessly. But solitude is not something to be feared. It's a space where you can truly meet yourself without distractions, where you can listen to your own thoughts and desires.

Loneliness may make you feel incomplete, but solitude reminds you that you're whole. It gives you the chance to reconnect with the parts of yourself that might have been overshadowed by the relationship. It's a time to nourish your soul, to explore your interests, and to grow into the person you're meant to be.

Learning to Be Alone Without Feeling Lonely

One of the hardest things after a breakup is learning to be okay with your own company. It's natural to feel the sting of loneliness, especially when you're used to sharing your life with someone else. But there's a difference between being alone and feeling lonely.

Being alone can be empowering. It's a reminder that you are enough, that you don't need someone else to complete you. Embracing solitude is about shifting your perspective. Instead of seeing it as a lack, view it as an opportunity—a chance to focus on yourself, to heal, and to grow.

Solitude is where you learn to love yourself, not out of necessity but out of genuine appreciation for who you are. It's in those quiet moments where you realize that you are your own best companion.

Rediscovering the Joy in Solitude

When you're in a relationship, your time is often intertwined with someone else's. Your days are filled with shared activities, conversations, and plans. After a breakup, it's easy to feel lost without those routines. But this is the perfect time to rediscover the things that bring you joy independently.

Think about the things you loved doing before the relationship. Maybe it was reading, painting, hiking, or simply spending time with your thoughts. Now is the time to dive back into those passions.

When you fill your life with activities that you enjoy, you start to appreciate your own company more and more.

Create rituals that are just for you—morning coffee in your favorite spot, evening walks with your thoughts, journaling by candlelight. These small moments of self-care build a sense of fulfillment that doesn't rely on anyone else.

The Power of Self-Reflection

Solitude offers the gift of introspection. In the stillness, you can reflect on your journey, your growth, and your dreams for the future. It's a time to ask yourself important questions: Who am I outside of this relationship? What do I truly want in life? What kind of person do I want to become?

This reflection isn't about dwelling on the past but about looking forward with clarity. Solitude allows you to reconnect with your innermost desires and values. It gives you the space to heal old wounds and to envision a future that aligns with your true self.

Finding Peace in Your Own Presence

The goal of embracing solitude isn't just about filling the time—it's about finding peace within yourself. When you're truly at peace with your own company, you discover that you don't need external validation to feel complete. You learn that you can be your own source of joy, comfort, and love.

This peace is what allows you to step into the next chapter of your life with confidence. It's what helps you build a future that is based on self-respect and self-love. When you're at peace in your own presence, you're no longer afraid of being alone because you realize that you are never truly lonely—you always have yourself.

The Peace in Solitude

In quiet rooms where shadows play,
I learned to be alone, to stay.
Not in the ache of empty space,
But in the warmth of my own embrace.

I found a friend within the still,
A heart that beats with gentle will.
No need for words, no need for more,
For in this quiet, my spirit soars.

Alone, I walk, yet not apart,
For in myself, I've found my heart.
No longer lost, no longer blind,
In solitude, my peace I find.

For when the world grows cold and gray,
I have my light to guide the way.
And in this space, I come to see,
That being alone sets my soul free.

Chapter 5: Rebuilding and Reinvesting in Yourself

A breakup can leave you feeling depleted, as though pieces of yourself were given away and never returned. But this chapter is about rebuilding—about taking all those fragmented pieces and crafting something beautiful. It's about turning the pain into purpose and focusing on your own growth. Rebuilding yourself is not just about moving on; it's about moving up and becoming the best version of who you can be.

Rebuilding Starts with Self-Care

Before you can grow, you need to heal. Self-care is more than just bubble baths and spa days—it's about nurturing your mind, body, and soul. After a breakup, it's easy to neglect your own needs while you're overwhelmed with emotion. But now is the time to prioritize yourself.

Start by treating yourself with the kindness and compassion you deserve. Allow yourself to rest when you're tired, eat well, and surround yourself with things that bring you peace. Healing isn't just about mending a broken heart—it's about restoring your energy and caring for yourself in a way that no one else can.

Set New Goals and Dreams

A breakup often leaves a void where shared dreams and goals once were. But instead of dwelling on what's lost, this is your opportunity to create new aspirations that are entirely your own. Ask yourself: What do I want to achieve? What are my passions, and what dreams have I put on hold?

Whether it's pursuing a career goal, learning a new skill, or diving into a creative project, setting new goals gives you something to look forward to. It redirects your energy from the past to the future. You're no longer just surviving—you're thriving by building the life you want for yourself.

Rediscovering Your Passions

Sometimes, in the midst of love, we let go of parts of ourselves to make space for someone else. Hobbies get forgotten, dreams get postponed, and passions fade. Now is the perfect time to rekindle those interests.

Think back to the activities that used to make you feel alive. Was there something you always wanted to try but never had the time or courage to pursue? Now is the time to go for it. Whether it's painting, writing, traveling, or anything else that sparks joy—rediscovering your passions helps you reconnect with your true self.

Building Healthy Habits

As you rebuild, it's important to establish routines that nurture your growth. This could mean adopting healthier habits like exercising regularly, meditating, journaling, or practicing mindfulness. Healthy habits create stability and structure, which are crucial when you're navigating the emotions of a breakup.

Small, consistent actions can lead to profound change over time. Even something as simple as dedicating 15 minutes a day to a new hobby or learning can bring about growth. These habits not only help you heal but also build a foundation for the person you're becoming.

Investing in Your Personal Growth

This chapter of your life is about more than just moving on—it's about evolving. Investing in yourself means continually seeking ways to grow and improve. This could mean reading books that inspire you, taking courses to expand your knowledge, or even seeking therapy or coaching if you need guidance.

Personal growth is a lifelong journey. Every step you take to better yourself not only helps you heal but also prepares you for the next chapter in your life. The person you're becoming is someone stronger, wiser, and more resilient than before.

Turning Pain into Purpose

One of the most powerful things you can do during this process is to transform your pain into purpose. Take what you've learned from the breakup and use it to fuel your growth. Your experiences can become the foundation of your strength and wisdom.

Remember, every challenge you overcome adds to your story. You're not defined by your heartbreak—you're defined by how you rise from it. Turning your pain into purpose is about finding meaning in what you've been through and using it to create a brighter future.

Rising from the Ashes

From the ashes of what once was mine,
I rise anew with purpose divine.
The tears that fell like endless rain,
Now water seeds of growth from pain.

I take each scar, each broken piece,
And craft a life of hope and peace.
For every wound that once was deep,
Is now the strength in which I leap.

This journey back is mine to own,
A path of light where I have grown.
For in this space, I've come to see,
I hold the power to set me free.

No longer bound by what has passed,
I rebuild with love that's meant to last—
A love for self, a love that's true,
A love that starts and ends with you.

Chapter 6: Embracing New Beginnings

Every ending paves the way for a new beginning. It's natural to feel a mix of fear and excitement when you step into the unknown, especially after a breakup. But life is full of cycles—endings and beginnings, loss and renewal. In this chapter, we'll explore how embracing new beginnings allows you to grow beyond what you thought was possible, giving you a chance to start again with a heart that is both wiser and stronger.

Letting Go to Make Space for the New

The first step in embracing new beginnings is letting go of what no longer serves you. This doesn't mean erasing memories or pretending the past didn't happen. Instead, it's about releasing the grip that past hurt and regret may have on you. You can honor the lessons learned while still opening yourself up to new experiences and possibilities.

Letting go is an act of courage. It requires you to trust that what lies ahead is worth more than what's left behind. When you clear away the emotional clutter, you create room for new opportunities, fresh connections, and a future that's not limited by the shadows of the past.

Finding Joy in the Unknown

Starting anew can be intimidating. The unknown is vast, and it's natural to cling to the familiar, even if it's no longer right for you. But in that space of uncertainty lies endless possibility. The unknown isn't just a void; it's a blank canvas where you can paint a life that's truer to who you are now.

When you approach new beginnings with curiosity rather than fear, you start to see them as exciting adventures. Each day becomes a chance to discover something new about yourself and the world. You don't have to have everything figured out—sometimes, the most beautiful journeys unfold when you allow life to surprise you.

Opening Yourself to New Connections

One of the hardest things after a breakup is imagining yourself opening up to someone new. It can feel like a betrayal of the love you once had, or you may fear getting hurt again. But opening up doesn't mean forgetting the past—it means honoring your growth and recognizing that you deserve happiness.

When you've healed, you'll find that you're drawn to new people who align with the person you've become. These new connections, whether romantic or platonic, are opportunities to experience love and companionship from a healthier, more authentic place. Allow yourself to be open to these connections without rushing or forcing anything. The right people will find their way into your life when you're ready.

Embracing Change as a Catalyst for Growth

New beginnings often come with change, and change can be uncomfortable. But it's through change that we grow. Every new chapter in life brings with it the chance to evolve, to step into a version of yourself that's more aligned with your truth. Change is the force that moves you forward, helping you shed old patterns and embrace new opportunities.

When you accept that change is a natural and necessary part of life, you stop resisting it and start flowing with it. You begin to see challenges as opportunities and obstacles as stepping stones. Every twist and turn becomes part of the beautiful unfolding of your story.

Visualizing the Life You Want

As you step into this new chapter, take time to visualize the life you want to create. What does happiness look like for you now? What kind of relationships, experiences, and goals do you want to pursue? By envisioning your ideal life, you give yourself a direction to move toward.

This is your time to dream big and set intentions that align with your desires. Whether it's focusing on your career, finding new hobbies, or deepening your self-love, these new beginnings are a chance to craft a life that reflects your values and aspirations.

Walking Forward with Hope

Hope is the light that guides you through uncertainty. It's what reminds you that even after the darkest nights, there are brighter days ahead. Embracing new beginnings is about holding on to that hope, even when you're unsure of what's next.

When you walk forward with hope, you're telling yourself that you believe in better days. You trust that life has more in store for you— more joy, more love, more growth. Hope allows you to step into the future with open arms, ready to receive all the good things that are waiting for you.

A New Chapter Begins

In every end, a seed is sown,
A chance to find a world unknown.
Though tears may fall and nights be long,
New dawns arise with hope so strong.

The past is done, its chapter closed,
Yet in its wake, a path unfolds.
For in the heart that dared to heal,
New dreams are born, and love is real.

So step ahead, though roads are new,
With faith in all that you'll pursue.
For life begins where fears are shed,
Where hope ignites, and light is spread.

Embrace the change, the fresh, the free—
This is your time, your destiny.
In every breath, a story starts,
A brand-new tale to fill your heart.

A Journey to Freedom and Self-Love

As we reach the end of this journey, remember that moving on is not just about leaving something behind—it's about embracing what lies ahead. You've walked through your pain, confronted your deepest emotions, and found the strength within yourself to heal. Every step you've taken has brought you closer to a new beginning, one that is filled with hope, love, and endless possibilities.

In life, heartbreak can feel like a storm that never ends, but even the fiercest storms eventually pass, giving way to clear skies and calm seas. Your heart, though it may have been bruised, is stronger now. It has learned to beat for itself again, to find joy in its own rhythm. The love you sought from others, you now know how to give to yourself—wholeheartedly and unconditionally.

This book was never just about moving on from a relationship. It was about rediscovering the incredible person you are. It was about finding joy in the simple moments, healing the wounds that time couldn't reach, and embracing your growth with grace and compassion.

A Message of Hope

You are not defined by your heartbreak, nor by the love you once lost. You are defined by how you chose to rise after falling, by the courage it took to rebuild yourself, and by the love you've learned to give to yourself. The story of your life is yours to write, and every ending is just a new beginning in disguise.

Your journey doesn't end here. As you close this chapter, let it be a reminder that every day is a chance to start anew. The strength you've cultivated, the love you've found within yourself, and the lessons you've learned will guide you as you step into the future.

You've come so far, and there's so much more ahead. Embrace it with an open heart, knowing that you are worthy of every bit of happiness and love that the world has to offer.